This Book Belongs To:

A joyful art!

Coloring isn't just about adding color to a page; it's about adding vibrancy to your life. Each stroke invites you into a world of wonder, where creativity blooms, stress melts away, and your mind finds peace.

The Tools are your choice

Your tools are an extension of your creative spirit, and the choice is entirely yours. Whether smooth, blendable pencils or bold, bright markers, the right materials will bring your visions to life. Keep your work crisp by placing a thick paper beneath the page you're coloring to avoid smudging or color bleed.

Make this experience yours! relax, create, and leave a lasting imprint of beauty on your life.

A joyful art

Coloring isn't just about adding color to a page, it's about adding vibrancy to your life. Each stroke invites you into a world of ... where ... stress melts away and your ... finds peace.

The Tools are your choice

Your tools are an extension of your creative spirit, and the choice is entirely yours. Whether smooth, blendable pencils or bold, bright markers, the right materials will bring your visions to life. Keep your work crisp by placing a thick paper beneath the page you're coloring to avoid smudging or color bleed.

Make this experience yours! relax, create, and leave a lasting imprint of beauty on your life.

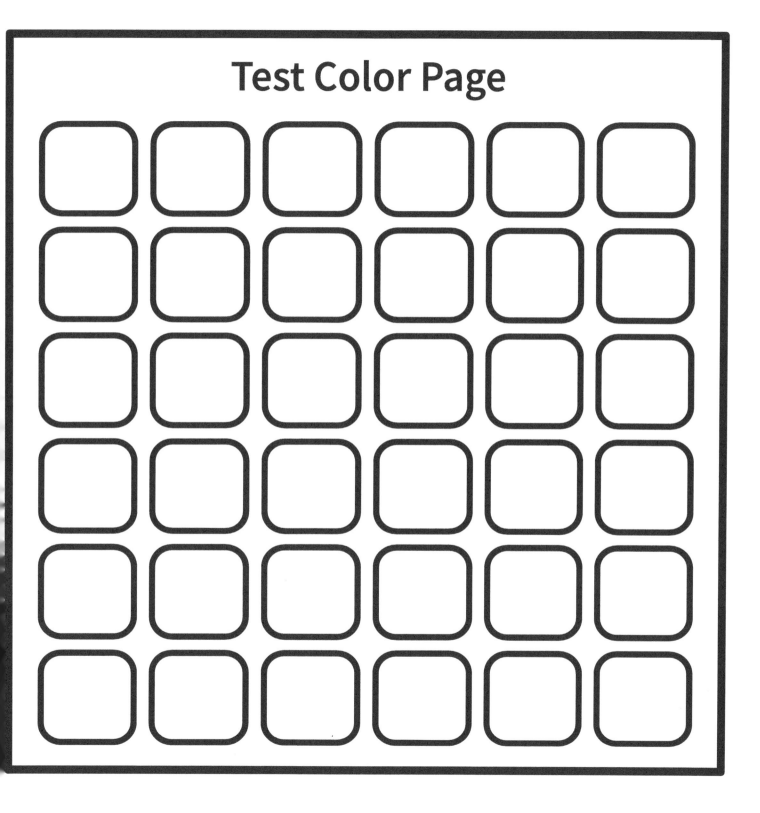

Test Color Page

Test Color Page

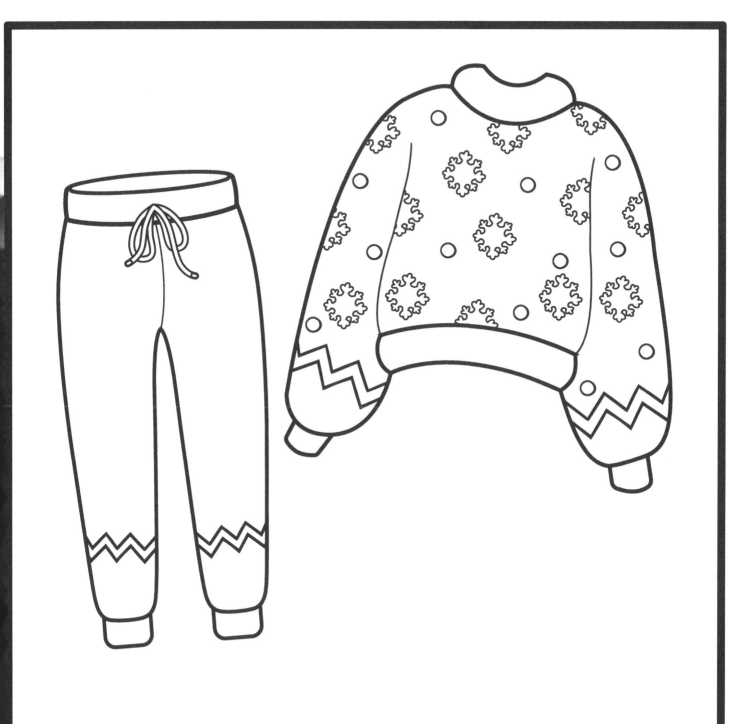

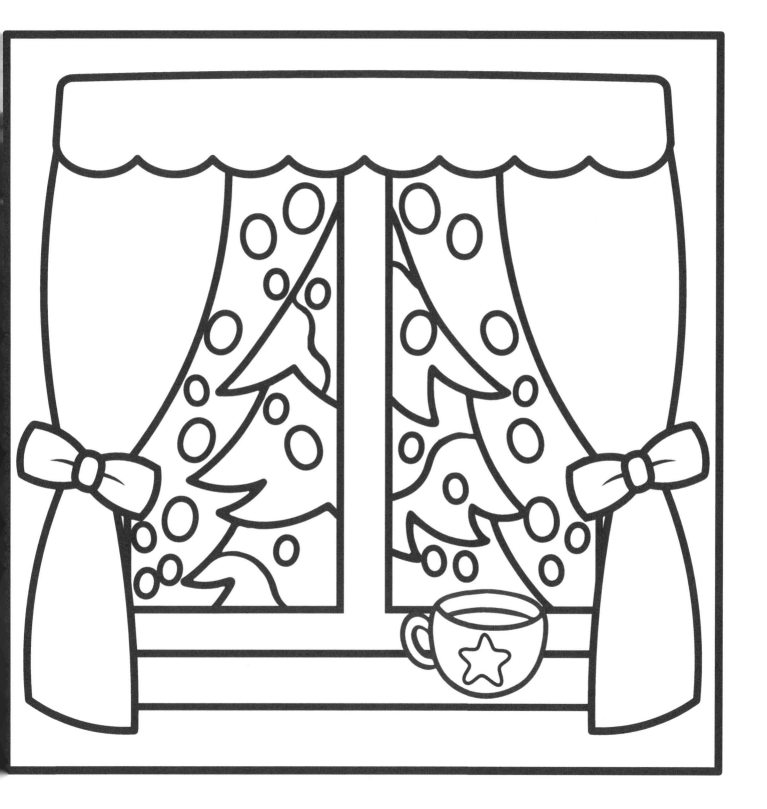

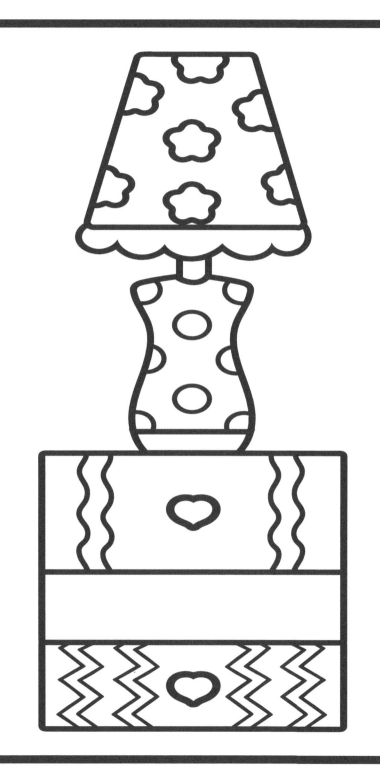

Made in United States
Cleveland, OH
12 December 2024

11748108R00039